# YOUTHWORK
## READY-TO-USE MEETING GUIDE
### VOLUME 1

# YOUTHWORK

## READY-TO-USE MEETING GUIDE
### VOLUME 1

*John Buckeridge*

*with contributions from*
*John Allan*

*Designed by Rachel Salter*

Kingsway Publications

Eastbourne

***To Dave Hanks:***
*a youth group leader during*
*my teenage years who was*
*my hero,*
*my mentor*
*and my friend.*

Copyright © Elm House Christian Communications Ltd. 1994

The right of Elm House Christian Communications to be identified as author of this work has been asserted by them in accordance with the Copyright, Designs and Patents Act 1988.

First Published 1994

All rights reserved.

Except for the photocopiable worksheets, which may be reproduced, no other part of this text may be reproduced, transmitted in any form or by any means, electronic or mechanical, including photocopy, recording, or any information storage and retrieval system, without permission in writing from the publisher.

ISBN 0 85476 511 5

Photos: Chris Gander, Luke Golobitsh, Jim Loring.
Illustrations: Ian Long
Design: Rachel Salter
Every Second Counts adaption devised by Peter Meadows for use in the main seminars at Spring Harvest 1994 and used with his permission.

Produced by Bookprint Creative Services PO Box 827, BN23 6NX, England, for KINGSWAY PUBLICATIONS LTD
Lottbridge Drove, Eastbourne, East Sussex BN23 6NT.
Printed in Great Britain.

# CONTENTS

**How to use the Guide**     6

**Publicity Ideas**     7

## READY-TO-USE MEETING GUIDE

**1. CHECK IT OUT –**     8
introduction to faith

**2. WHAT IS GOD LIKE? –**     10
the character of God

**3. SIN –**     12
God's solution to our problems

**4. WHO IS JESUS? –**     14
fully human and divine

**5. HOLY SPIRIT –**     16
fruits, gifts and work of the Spirit

**6. WE ARE FAMILY –**     18
the church

**7. WORLD'S BESTSELLER –**     20
the Bible

**8. PRAYER –**     22
communicating with God

**9. FORGIVENESS –**     24
forgiving others as God forgives us

**10. DOUBTS –**     26
a positive force for growth

# Introduction

**T**his material has been designed to be used with 12 to 16-year-olds. That doesn't mean it can't work with younger or older youngsters, but then it will probably need to be adapted and changed.

No two groups of young people are the same, therefore although these 10 meeting plans are designed to be 'ready to use', you will need to adapt some of the material to make it work really well with own particular group of young people.

The 10 sessions can be used in a series, but will work just as well as individual units. In fact you may find that some of the units contain too much for just one week. The key thing is to adapt and personalise the material to take into account your own gifting, available resources and the needs of your young people.

Most of the units include icebreaker games, discussion starters and other interaction elements. It is important to avoid too much 'chalk and talk' style teaching. Young people learn best through a mix of learning elements.

The reproducible sheets vary in form and content. They use a mix of styles to stimulate Bible study, discussion and reflection on the meeting theme. You are free to photocopy these for local church use. This does not apply to large-scale events where over 100 people are expected.

As well as the reproducible sheets there is also a publicity page with illustrations for you to use to publicise the first meeting in this term-long series.

Please do prepare well. Although this book is designed to take some of the hard work and hassle out of preparation, you will still need to read through the meeting plan at least a couple of days beforehand. This will give you time to collect any props or other equipment you need as well as Bibles, pens and copies of the repro-sheet.

This book (one of a series of four) was written in response to requests to me at YOUTH**WORK** magazine from youth leaders/workers. The call was for more of the Ready-To-Use Meeting pages from the magazine - well, here there are! I'd be interested to get your feedback, both positive and negative, so any further books can take your comments into consideration. Write to me at YOUTH**WORK** Magazine, 37 Elm Road, New Malden, Surrey KT3 3HB. If you haven't seen a copy of YOUTH**WORK** or would like to subscribe, check out the advertisement on page 28.

*John Buckeridge*

**PUBLICITY PAGE**

**G**et your meeting noticed by using the ready-to-photocopy artwork below to promote the first week of this term-long series of meetings. Simply add the details of venue and time and photocopy onto paper or thin coloured card. This image can be shrunk in size to use as a personal invite or expanded to poster size to pin onto a notice board at church, school, youth club etc.

# Check It Out

BRING AN EMPTY STOMACH AND A QUESTIONING MIND

FEED YOUR GUT and FEED YOUR MIND

**Join us ↓**

INVESTIGATE THE CLAIMS OF CHRISTIANITY 4 YOURSELF

# CHECK IT OUT

**MEETING AIM:**
To encourage young people to begin to investigate the Christian faith.

## TASTE AND SEE (10 mins)
Buy at least eight packets of different flavoured crisps. Before the young people arrive empty each packet into a bowl and number the bowls one to eight. Keep a careful record of which flavour is in which bowl.

As the young people arrive give them each a pen and small sheet which lists the eight flavours. They must correctly match up each flavour with the correct number. Make sure you buy some similar flavours such as Beef, Marmite, and Beef and Onion to add to the confusion - plus of course the old favourites like Salt and Vinegar and Cheese and Onion.

## SUPER SARNIES (10-15 mins)
Some strange combinations of foods work well together. A banana and jam sandwich may sound disgusting, but it tastes great! This game provides a chance to experiment with 15 different food flavours.

Give everyone the chance to make two experimental sandwiches with a maximum of three filling mixtures in each.

Suggested fillings are; strawberry jam, marmite, cheddar cheese slices, cream cheese, honey, brown sugar, chocolate spread, slices of banana, tuna, sliced tomato, peanut butter, raisins, mustard, cold sliced sausage, shredded lettuce, walnuts, cress, luncheon meat slices, onion rings, sweetcorn, finely sliced celery. Don't forget you will also need sufficient bread and margarine.

Encourage individuals to come up with creative names for their new sarnie combos.

Appoint a taste test committee of three young people and a leader/helper to decide on the tastiest combination and the weirdest taste mixture.

If you feel like being generous, give a McDonalds meal voucher to the maker of the best sarnie.

## TASTE AND SEE (5 mins)
Read Psalm 34:8-10 in a modern translation.
**SAY:** 'I believe it is important that people think through for themselves and test out what the Christian faith is all about.
'Just as you needed to taste each crisp before you could decide on its flavour - and how seemingly weird combinations of sandwich filling sometimes tasted good when you checked them out - in the same way, it's easier to come to a conclusion about whether Christianity is true or not by checking it out for yourself. Many people dismiss it without investigating the facts, reading the Bible, praying to God etc.

## MY LIFE SO FAR... (15 mins)
Hand out copies of the sheet opposite and a pen/pencil. Ask everyone to fill in the boxes with the significant things that happened to them at that age/stage of development. Allow about five minutes for this.

Allow time for everyone to feedback what they wrote. Use this as a way to get to know your group better.

## WALKING ON WATER (15 mins)
Turn down the lights and/or draw the curtains so the room is darkish, but light enough for you to read.

Explain that you are going to read out a story from the Bible and appoint everyone a character from the story. For every six people in the group appoint one to be Jesus, one to be Peter and the rest assorted disciples.

Then carefully explain the context of the reading and take time to encourage each person to 'get into their character from the story'.

Read Matthew 14:22-34 slowly - pausing between verses to allow the impact of the story to have an effect. You may want to read it through a second time. Then ask the group to describe how they felt and thought during the story, in particular get them to verbalise:
- How the disciples felt when Jesus first appeared.
- How Peter felt when he stepped out of the boat.
- The disciple's reaction to Peter's decision to get out of the boat and what the other disciples expected to happen next.
- Peter's reaction when he started walking on water.
- Jesus' reaction to Peter's decision to get out of the boat.
- Why Peter started to sink.
- What Jesus was thinking when Peter was sinking.
- The thoughts/reactions of all the characters in the story once everyone was back on dry land.
- Do the disciples think of Jesus in a different way following this miracle? If so, how?

## MODERN-DAY MIRACLES (10 mins)
Ask if any of them have ever had a prayer answered, seen a miracle, asked God for healing, etc. Encourage open discussion and sharing.

Most people have prayed to God at a moment of crisis or difficulty. John McCarthy, a British journalist kidnapped in Lebanon in the 1980s, asked for help from God during a particularly bleak moment during his long captivity. He did not consider himself a Christian, or religious, but in the book *Some Other Rainbow* he records 'The next instant I was standing up, surrounded by a warm bright light. I was dancing full of joy. In the space of a minute, despair had vanished, replaced by boundless optimism.'

Most times when people pray a 'God help me' type prayer, even if God answers they tend to forget about him.

Emphasise that God is interested in developing a relationship with us, rather than only being contacted when we are in an emergency.

## BEEN THERE, DONE IT (10 mins)
Invite a Christian to come and briefly share their testimony about how they came to faith in Jesus (alternatively it could be one of the young people or you). Encourage the person to be totally honest, and open it up for questions from the young people.
The testimony does not necessarily have to be a highly dramatic, 'I used to be a drug-taking, sex-mad, rock 'n' roll star' account, to make a big impression.

Conclude by saying that hearing about someone's personal experience of God isn't conclusive evidence but it is important and it should be carefully considered.

### OPTIONAL EXTRA
Pray and look for opportunities during this evening or at a later date to ask individuals who are not Christians what it would take for them to believe in God and become a Christian/or alternatively what is stopping them!

This needs to be delicately and diplomatically put, but could result in a significant conversation about their struggles, doubts or problems about the Christian faith.

# THE STORY SO FAR

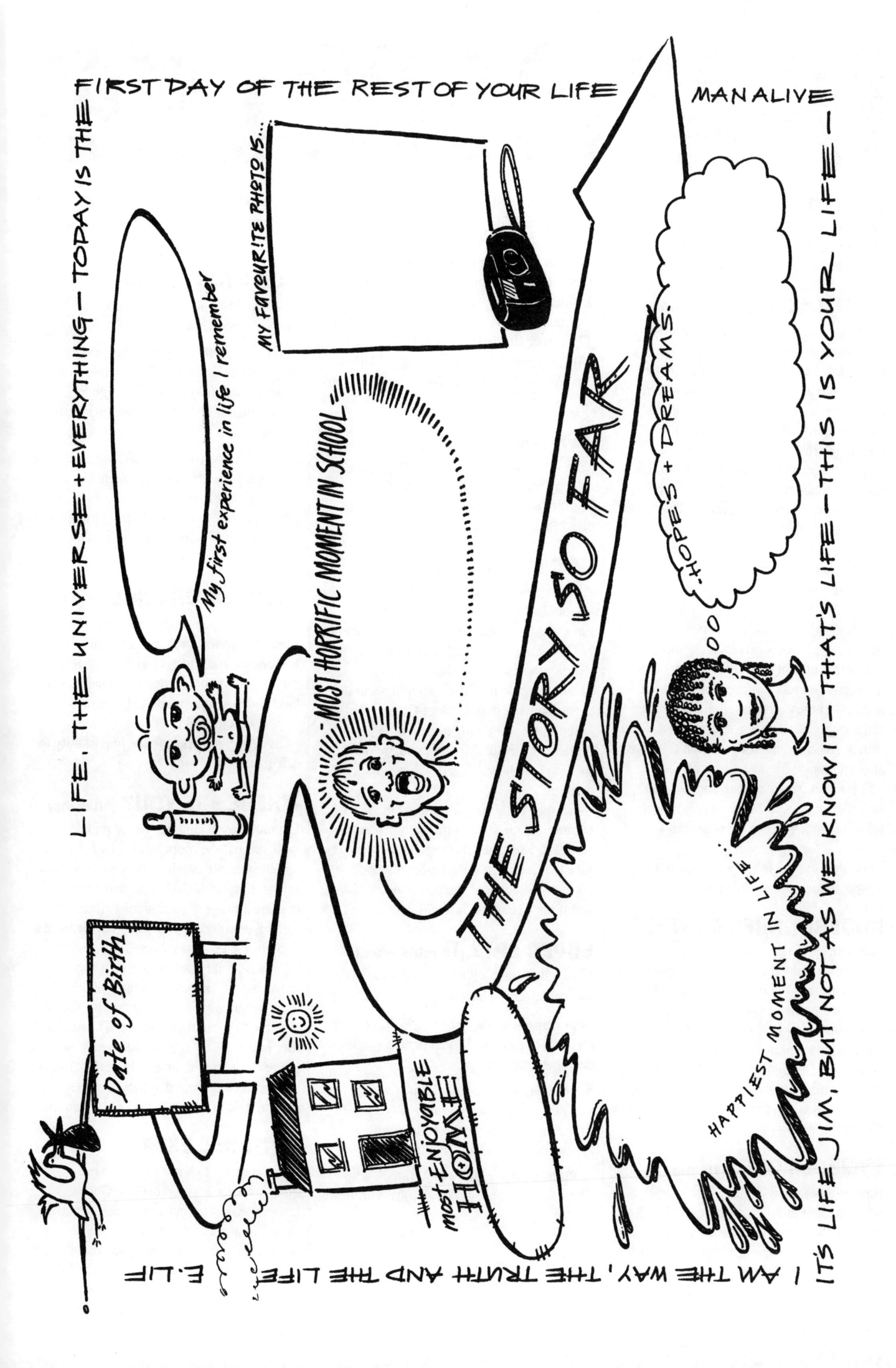

FIRST DAY OF THE REST OF YOUR LIFE

MAN ALIVE

LIFE, THE UNIVERSE + EVERYTHING — TODAY IS THE

MY FAVOURITE PHOTO IS...

My first experience in life I remember

Date of Birth

MOST HORRIFIC MOMENT IN SCHOOL

HOPE'S + DREAMS.

most ENJOYABLE HOME

HAPPIEST MOMENT IN LIFE....

E. LIF

I AM THE WAY, THE TRUTH AND THE LIFE

IT'S LIFE JIM, BUT NOT AS WE KNOW IT — THAT'S LIFE — THIS IS YOUR LIFE —

# WHAT IS GOD LIKE?

## MEETING AIM:
To identify young people's perceptions of the nature of God and present the biblical view of him as a real, living, supreme person.

## SPOT THE CELEB (10 mins)
Tear out photographs of celebrities from magazines and on a photocopier enlarge or shrink them to A4 size, then transfer the image onto an OHP acetate. You will need to use special acetates designed for this purpose - ordinary ones will melt in the photocopier!

Split the group into two equal teams and then announce that you will slowly reveal a picture of someone well known. They need to correctly identify the celebrity.

Put the first acetate with a backing mask onto the screen, then gradually draw back the masking paper to reveal more and more of the face.

As soon as someone from one of the teams shouts 'stop', you stop revealing more of the face and the team has 10 seconds to identify the person correctly (accept only the first answer). If they are wrong, the other team can see the whole face for their guess. Only if they guess wrong does the first team have another chance to identify the celeb.

This means that if a team shouts 'stop' before they are sure, they run the risk of handing the answer to the other team on a plate.

Use this and the following game to focus on the theme of identification.

## KNOBBLY KNEE CONTEST (10 mins)
Ask for six volunteers - four lads, two girls. The girls are taken out of the room while the lads sit on a row of chairs and roll up their right trouser leg to above the knee.

The girls are blindfolded and led in one at a time. A helper guides them down the line of lads while they touch each knee in turn. The girls then attempt to identify which knee belongs to whom.

## SYMBOLS QUIZ (10 mins)
Hand out pens and copies of the sheet opposite, and ask the group to work (as individuals or in small teams - you choose) through the symbols identifying what they each represent. Emphasise that they should not begin to complete the second half of the sheet (God Is...) even if they finish the quiz early.

ANSWERS: 1) Do not Bleach 2) British Telecom 3) HMV 4) Water 5) Mercedes-Benz 6) Head 7) Warm Iron 8) Dispose of Litter in Bin 9) Treble Clef 10) Midland Bank 11) UniChem 12) The Body Shop 13) Mercury Communications 14) Apple Computer 15) Birds Eye 16) Abbey National 17) Warner Brothers 18) Wella 19) Michelin 20) Recyclable 21) Yellow Pages 22) Pure New Wool 23) Renault 24) Norwich Union 25) Lacoste

## ASK (3 mins)
Why are symbols so widely used?
(They represent a larger piece of information - they symbolise something, eg white flag = surrender.)

## GOD IS... (15 mins)
Ask the group to draw a symbol on the bottom half of the photocopied sheet to represent their understanding/belief/unbelief of God. They are not allowed to use any words, lettering or numbers. The picture/graphic they draw should accurately represent what they think of God, eg a cloud to represent something hidden or mysterious. Emphasise that you are not looking for a work of art! Allow three minutes.

Ask the young people to show the rest of the group their symbol picture - group to feedback what they think the symbol means, *then* the 'artist' to say whether anyone correctly interpreted their symbolic drawing, and if not to explain it themselves.

## SUPER SPY? (10 mins max.)
Give a short talk which identifies the main ideas that people have about God.

**Super Spy** - A nosy parker who has his eye on everyone so that he can punish you if you do something wrong.

**Santa Claus** - A kindly old man who gives you things if you are vaguely good. A bit out of touch, but someone to be honoured on special occasions like Christmas.

**A Blob** - Not a person but a 'force', a bit like lightning. Not someone you could form a relationship with or get to know personally.

**The Doctor** - Someone to call on in an emergency, but ignore when everything is going OK.

The Bible teaches that God is a real, living person who is a spirit. In small groups examine what else the Bible says God is like.

## GOD STUDY (15 mins)
1) **ASK:** From what sources do we get our ideas of what God is like?

2) **READ:** John 14:5-10. What two things do we learn about what God is like from these verses? (God is a father figure, God made himself known to us as a man called Jesus).

3) **LIST:** as many qualities/characteristics of God that you can which are mentioned in the Bible, back this up with Bible verses wherever you can. If a group is struggling, point them to Psalm 8 and Psalm 24 for ideas.

## IN MY EXPERIENCE (5 mins)
Prearrange with one of your young people, someone from church, one of your co-leaders (or you!) to give a short, three-minute testimony of their relationship with God and how they relate to him as a father/supreme being.

Give the young people the opportunity to ask questions.

## WHERE ARE YOU? (10 mins)
Conclude by asking the young people to walk around the room and find a road sign which symbolises where they are at in their relationship with God. You will need to prepare a range of road signs beforehand (drawn or enlarged on a photocopier from a copy of the Highway Code).

Each person brings back a sign and explains in what way the sign symbolises their experience of God, eg the 'No Entry' sign could mean they feel cut off from God, the 'bumpy road' sign could signify they are going through a rough patch, or the '70mph' sign could represent that they feel they are making fast progress in their Christian life.

## OPTIONAL EXTRA
Ask the group to write down the one question they would most like God to answer. Ask different group members to take it in turn to 'play God' and try to answer the question. Emphasise that it isn't wrong to ask God hard questions, and that even if we don't get an answer now, one day if we go to heaven, we will get the opportunity to ask God face to face.

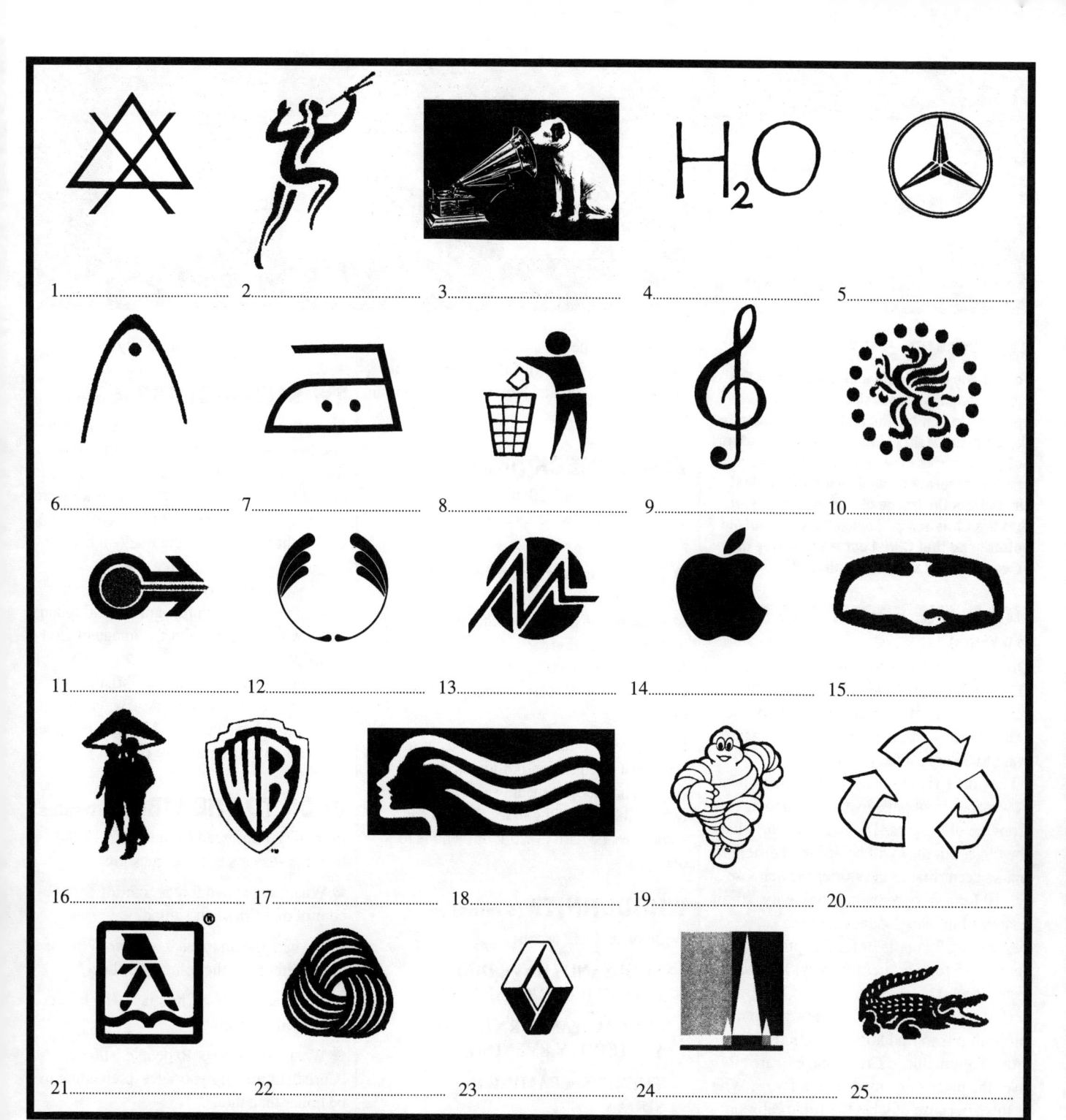

1. ..........................
2. ..........................
3. ..........................
4. $H_2O$
5. ..........................
6. ..........................
7. ..........................
8. ..........................
9. ..........................
10. ..........................
11. ..........................
12. ..........................
13. ..........................
14. ..........................
15. ..........................
16. ..........................
17. ..........................
18. ..........................
19. ..........................
20. ..........................
21. ..........................
22. ..........................
23. ..........................
24. ..........................
25. ..........................

God is...

# SIN

## MEETING AIM
To help the group gain a clearer idea of the Bible's teaching about sin, the way it operates in human life, and God's solution to the problem. Main points: that sin is a nature, not just a series of wrong actions; that sin can be corporate as well as individual; that sin distorts the image of God in human life; that the Christian still possesses a sinful old nature; and that Christ came to destroy the power of sin by sacrificing himself.

## HOLD THE FRONT PAGE (10 mins)
Divide the group into teams of four or five. Give each a pile of old newspapers, a pair of scissors, some glue and a photocopy of the Daily Blast worksheet opposite (you may want to enlarge it to A3 format).

They have five minutes to make their own newspaper front page by taking clippings from the old papers. They can include what they like, but they will be awarded different marks according to the stories they choose (eg 10 for a story of human depravity, 20 for a story of human goodness, 5 for a pessimistic forecast, 10 for an optimistic forecast, 5 for a crime/war story, 10 for a love story...).

This exercise should show how much more difficult it is to find hopeful, optimistic stories of goodness. Crime and evil are all over the place in many different forms. Why is this? Because of what the Bible calls sin.

## THE GRAVITY TRAIN (5 mins)
Ask people to shout out the first word that crosses their mind when the word 'sin' is mentioned. Usually they will come up with a list of actions: thieving, adultery, murder etc. Make the point that these are just some of the *results* of sin - the fruit on the tree. The root of it is an evil bias fixed deep in the human nature.

Stand one volunteer on a chair, grasping one end of a broomstick. Another volunteer stands on the ground, behind a line drawn two feet in front of the chair, grasping the other end of the broomstick. Tell them that on no account are they to let go of the stick, but by twisting and pulling, the first volunteer is to try and pull the second over the line. The second has to try and pull the first off the chair.

Most times the person on the chair will lose. Gravity is a powerful force pulling us downwards and that's how the Bible says sin operates in our lives.

## BIBLE CHECK (10 mins)
Read Romans 7:15-20, then get them to discuss the following questions in small groups:

● What are the two bizarre results that sin produces (v15)?
● What is it inside people that produces these results (v17-18)?
● What would Paul have said to people who claimed, 'I try my best - nobody can do more'?

Paul goes on to talk about sin in us as a 'law' just like gravity, pulling us down (v23). That doesn't mean we're not responsible for giving in to it! But it can sometimes be hard to work out who is to blame...

## WHODUNNIT? (5 mins)
Write on an OHP acetate:

**THOUSANDS HAVE DIED IN FORMER YUGOSLAVIA**

**MY TEA WAS BURNT YESTERDAY EVENING**

**THERE IS A FAMINE IN SUDAN**

**I TOLD A LIE**

**HENRY WAS ABUSED AS A CHILD AND NOW ABUSES CHILDREN HIMSELF**

ASK: who is responsible for each of these evil things? Some are simple to work out - others are more difficult.

Allow people to argue for a while, then say; sometimes you can't just find one individual to blame - sometimes blame has to be shared. Sometimes the evil is in the very structures of society, like when a repressive government denies basic human rights, or when a multinational corporation oppresses poor people to make massive profits for its shareholders.

That's the trouble with sin it spreads everywhere. Theologians speak about 'total depravity' - which means that every human activity is twisted and tainted by sin.

## TWISTED PICTURE (5 mins)
Show the group a slide picture (of anything you like). When it's projected, you see on the wall a perfect representation of what's on the film. In the same way, when we were created, we were a perfect representation of God's character - we were made in his image.

Now twist the lens. The picture becomes blurred and finally unrecognisable. Explain, that's what sin does, blur the image of God in people.

When someone becomes a Christian, the image of God is renewed. A new nature arrives which we never had before. But does that mean our struggles are over?

## BACK TO THE BIBLE (10 mins)
In small groups, read Romans 8:5-11 and look for answers to these questions:

● What are the two forces fighting for control of a Christian's mind?

● We can give in to each of them. What is the difference in the results we'll get?

● If you are really a Christian, which force is invincible - and why?

● What's the answer to people who say, 'Christians are all hypocrites, pretending to be holier than thou'?

## SIN BONFIRE (10 mins)
Give everyone paper and a pen. Ask them to think back over the past week and mark a tick on the paper for each time they can remember doing something sinful. Stress that they won't have to show this to anyone else! Then fold up all the papers and collect them in a heap on a Pyrex dish, and read out Hebrews 9:26b-28. Explain that we are sinners and will always be until we reach heaven, but that Easter won our freedom (1 Peter 3:18). God will not condemn us for our sins, or leave us powerless to overcome temptation.

Then, slowly and wordlessly, squirt lighter fuel over the pile of paper and set it alight. As it burns, pray together, thanking Jesus for dying on the cross and the liberation from sin's slavery that it brings.

# THE DAILY BLAST

**FISHMART**

Come and try our fresh, tasty fish

Open every week day from 2 - 10pm

14 Cod's Wallop, Fishguard.

# WHO IS JESUS?

## MEETING AIM:
To introduce Jesus as a historical person who was both fully human and fully divine, and someone who is very different from the popular but largely mythical Christmas card/stained-glass image.

## IDENTIKIT (10 mins)
Use this as an opening game or even as an intro game (as people arrive at the venue for the meeting). You will need to collect at least 25 photographs of very well-known pop-stars, sportsmen/women, TV/film personalities/actors, etc. Because their faces are so well known make it a bit harder to identify the person by cutting out just a small part of their face (eg eyes and nose) and then display these around the walls of the venue/room. Beside each part of face put a number. With a pad and pencil, the young people need to identify the stars from the photofit section of face shown.

Give a suitably crazy prize for the winner(s) eg, painting by numbers set, eye make-up kit, rubber face mask, eye patch, whodunnit detective novel.

## MEEK AND MILD? (10 mins)
Collect a selection of pictures and illustrations depicting Jesus. These could include Christmas cards, postcards of oil paintings, religious pictures and statutes. Ask the young people to comment on the pictures and give an opinion of the sort of person these images portray.

Sum up by making the point that Jesus is considered by many to have been a wimpy, white-faced, blue-eyed man who wore a white sheet and ended up a victim. Make the point that the Bible does not portray him like that at all!

## SPOT THAT MAN (15 mins)
Provide photocopies of the worksheet opposite, give 10 minutes for the activity and five minutes for feedback. You could also pin some/all of the completed worksheets onto the wall.

## JESUS FAX QUIZ (5 mins)
Ask the group to divide up into teams of three. Then read out the following statements about Jesus. Allow 10 seconds' discussion in their threes then they need to decide if the statement is true or false. Ask them to keep a score and at the end ask them if they got more right than wrong.

**1)** Jesus has several half-brothers and sisters *(T)*.

**2)** Mary was no more than 19 when she gave birth to Jesus *(T)* [Not proven, but highly likely to be].

**3)** Instead of a cot the baby Jesus slept in an animal feeding trough *(T)*.

**4)** During his lifetime on earth Jesus travelled in a part of the Middle East no bigger than Wales *(T)*.

**5)** Jesus once told a story about 10 virgins *(T)*.

**6)** Jesus predicted the rise and fall of communism *(F)*.

**7)** There is more proof that Julius Caesar existed than Jesus *(F)*.

**8)** During his lifetime Jesus spent five times as many years working with wood as with people *(T)*.

**9)** At the time of his death Jesus had about 3,000 followers *(F)* [around 100].

**10)** Every day around 70,000 more people decide to become followers of Jesus *(T)*.

## WHAT WOULD YOU DO? (10 mins)
Ask your group what they would do in the following situations, then get them to check out the Bible verses.

**1)** You are sitting on a park bench talking with your mates, when a group of little kids sit down and start listening in and then joining in on your conversation. Your friends tell the little kids to get lost. What do you do?
*Now read Mark 10:13-16.*

**2)** A group of lads about your age or older start picking on a girl three years younger than them. She is on her own. The lads ask you to join the bullying or risk getting picked on yourself. What do you do?
*Now read John 8:1-11.*

**3)** One of your best friends is spotted by a gang of people who don't like you. Your friend tells them he is not your friend, in fact he hardly even knows you. He shouts and swears to make his point. Then you get badly beaten up by this gang. The next time you see your (supposed) friend he wants to hang around with you and be your best mate. What do you do?
*Now read Matthew 26:31-35; Mark 14:66-72; John 21:15-19.*

## FULLY HUMAN - FULLY GOD (10 mins)
**SAY:** 'Christians believe that Jesus was the Son of God and that he was at the same time fully human (cut him and he bleeds) AND fully God (perfect and holy).'

Divide your young people into two, hand out Bibles in a modern translation (preferably the same one) and get one group to read out loud the passages which highlight Jesus' humanness, and the second group to read out the passages which reveal that Jesus' was the Son of God. After each reading, ask the group what human or divine qualities the reading demonstrates.

| HUMAN | DIVINE |
|---|---|
| Matthew 26:36-38 | John 10:30-33 |
| John 4:5-8 | Mark 7:27-30 |
| John 11:28-36 | John 11:38-48 |
| Matthew 27:45-46 | Matthew 27:50-54 |

## YOUR STORY (5 mins)
Finish the session by telling the young people what Jesus means to you. Talk about how you became a Christian, what convinced you to follow Jesus and give examples of what following Christ has meant (both in terms of cost and benefits) in your life.

## OPTIONAL EXTRAS
**1)** Show part of the *Jesus* video (available from Scripture Press/International Films for £19.95). This 120-minute film follows the life of Jesus. Alternatively you could hire or buy the much acclaimed *Jesus of Nazareth* which starred Robert Powell as Jesus and was directed by Franco Zeferrelli (available from most video stockists).

**2)** Get your group to make a banner which portrays one of the characteristics of Jesus. Alternatively, get them to draw/paint a Bayeux tapestry-style collage on a roll(s) of paper/wallpaper/backing paper for wallpaper. Display their work in the group/club room, at church, and at the next March For Jesus nearest you (you may need to carve up the long tapestry for this last idea!).

The religious leaders mostly hated Jesus and towards the end of this three-year preaching tour they wanted to kill him. Imagine that you are compiling a wanted poster for Jesus. From the gospel accounts and using a bit of discretion build up a profile of the man Jesus, eg skin colour, age, habits, regular places he visits, people he mixes with, aliases or other names, family background, occupation, likes and dislikes, personality/behaviour characteristics, plus any other relevant data.

# WANTED
## DEAD OR ALIVE

### Jesus of Nazareth

**If you see this man report his whereabouts at once to the Roman army or religious secret police force. On no account should you approach this man - he is highly dangerous and powerful.**

### REWARD:
**For information leading to arrest and successful conviction the religious authorities will pay**
### 30 pieces of silver!

# HOLY SPIRIT

## MEETING AIM:
To teach on aspects of the person and work of the Holy Spirit and to emphasise the importance of both the gifts and the fruit of the Holy Spirit. Also to encourage people to ask God to fill them, grow in the fruit and receive and exercise gifts of the Holy Spirit.

**N.B. There is a lot of material in this session and you may want to divide it into two weeks.**

## BALLOON BREATH (10 mins)
Give everyone a balloon and ask them to blow it up so big that it bursts! After the pops of bursting balloons and laughter die down introduce the session with 'This week we are going to be looking at God's Holy Spirit. In the Old Testament the word used for "spirit" is "ruach" which literally means "breath" or "wind". When you breathed into your balloons they had life and energy. In the same way when the "ruach" or the Spirit of God fills us we have God's life and energy to live fulfilled and godly lives.

'The Bible also teaches that the Holy Spirit is not a force, but a person. He is part of God (Father, Son, Holy Spirit) and we are told not to grieve him and make him sad by stopping him work in our lives or by doing evil (Ephesians 4:30).'

## NAME THAT FRUIT (10 mins)
Peel and cut into cubes a selection of fruits. You will need one cube of each fruit for everyone present. Have everyone sitting down in a pitch black room or have them blindfold.

Then feed a cube of the first fruit (eg, melon) to everyone. The lights go up for 10 seconds to allow them to write down what they thought the fruit was. Then turn off the lights and bring in the next fruit.

Use between six and 10 fruits in total, and be sure to include one or two unusual/exotic fruits as well as apple, banana, satsuma etc.

## FRUIT OF THE SPIRIT (7 mins)
**SAY:** 'God's Holy Spirit is involved in our lives. He helps us to come to faith in Jesus, and when we become a Christian he lives inside us. He gives us the power to be Jesus' followers and St Paul writes that he encourages us to grow like fruit. Fruit takes time to mature into ripeness. In the same way as God's Spirit works in us, we will gradually become more and more mature - like Jesus. Paul lists what this fruit is in Galatians 5:22-26. We all need these qualities in our lives.'

**ASK:** the group to complete section one of the worksheet.

## FILLED WITH THE SPIRIT (3 mins)
**SAY:** 'Although the Holy Spirit lives in us when we become Christians, God wants us to receive him in fullness and power.'

**READ:** Acts 8:14-17 as an example of people who believed in Jesus but had not been filled with the Holy Spirit. Make the point that this is an ongoing process. God wants us to go on asking him to fill us with his Spirit (Ephesians 5:18).

## GET THE BALANCE (10 mins)
The props you need for this game are: two or more kitchen balance scales and a large number of parcels of differing weights.

Ideally you need a pair of scales for every four people. Prepare a large number of parcels (at least 20) which should all be a slightly different weight from each other, up to 3lbs in weight.

By putting different things in different parcels - eg paper, a brick, a balloon, they will differ in shape as well as weight. Finally make up two parcels which are identical in weight. Then number each parcel clearly with a different number.

The game requires each group to attempt to discover the two parcels which are identical in weight. They do this by selecting two parcels from the pile and weighing them on the scale to see if they balance. If they think they have the perfect match they shout out the two numbers to you, to discover if they are right. At the end of the game say: 'Some Christians emphasise the importance of the fruit of the Spirit, while others emphasise the gifts of the Spirit. The truth is that both are of equal importance and need to be kept in balance. We need to be demonstrating the fruit of the Spirit (love, joy, peace, patience etc) and we need to be exercising the gifts of the Spirit (prophecy, tongues, faith etc).

## FLOUR FEAR (15 mins)
Fill a small round pudding bowl with flour. Use a knife to level off the flour in the bowl, pressing it down well. Then put a large flat plate or stiff piece of card onto the bowl. Turn the bowl over and carefully lift the bowl up so that the flour stays in a moulded shape. Then carefully put a chocolate finger biscuit into the top of the flour pie.

The group take it in turn to shave a piece off the edge of the flour with a blunt knife without causing the finger biscuit to slip/fall off. The daring slice a large segment away.

This continues with the fear factor of failure mounting as the flour pie gets smaller and smaller, until someone disturbs the biscuit. They must then pick out the biscuit from the crumbled pie with their teeth. This isn't easy, especially if someone helpfully pushes their head into the flour at the wrong moment!

Talk about the game and how the tension and apprehension grew. Then explain that a lot of Christians are apprehensive or even fearful of the Holy Spirit, and in particular the 'Gifts of the Spirit'. Ask the group what sort of things people are afraid of concerning the Holy Spirit, and in particular, the gifts.

## GIFTS OF THE SPIRIT (7 mins)
**SAY:** 'Although the Holy Spirit is himself a gift, he wants to give us more. The gifts of the Spirit are for every Christian and Paul says we should eagerly want them (1 Corinthians 14:1). The different gifts are listed in 1 Corinthians 12:1-11 and are designed to build us up in our faith and to build up the church.

'Sometimes people are afraid of these gifts. They are afraid that maybe they will lose control when the Holy Spirit fills them or gives them a gift. This is not the case. The Holy Spirit is gentle and will not force us to do anything we don't want to do.

**ASK:** the group to complete section three of the worksheet.

## QUESTIONS, QUESTIONS (10-20 mins)
You may want to give a whole extra week to explaining the use and function of the gifts of the Spirit described in 1 Corinthians 12:4-11. If not, briefly make the following points and allow time for questions about what you have covered so far.

☛ **Wisdom** - not logic, but supernatural wisdom - an insight into a problem that seemed to have no answer.

☛ **Word of knowledge** - God revealing something about a person/situation.

☛ **Faith** - confidence in God's ability to

heal/speak/do something out of the ordinary.
- **Healing** - supernatural healing in body, emotions or mind.
- **Miracles** - dramatic signs and deeds.
- **Prophecy** - spoken to strengthen, encourage and comfort. Sometimes predicts a future event. Can take various forms, eg, vision, spoken word, drama. Must always be carefully tested and considered. Should always be in line with existing revelation (Bible).
- **Discerning Spirits** - noticing the presence of evil spirits.
- **Tongues** - ability to speak to God in a language you haven't learned. Can be used in praise and/or intercession. Two areas of use: i) Private - helps you grow spiritually (1 Corinthians 4:2), ii) Public - spoken out loud which then requires interpretation.
- **Interpretation of tongues** - able to explain a message in tongues given in public. Not a translation, but gives the basic message/heart of what is said. A tongue in private to God does not need interpretation.

**NB -** The gifts often work together, eg Ananias (Acts 9:1-18) who used prophecy, visions, healing and faith together.
– We need to use and practise the gifts to become more fluent.

## BEING FILLED

These things can be a block and prevent God from filling us with the Holy Spirit. Therefore they need to be confessed/dealt with: ● Not a Christian. ● Unconfessed sin. ● Feelings of fear, hurt or rejection. ● Previous involvement with occult, eg ouija, tarot, levitation.

Allow a moment of silence for people to get right with God, confess sin etc.

In an atmosphere of worship pray – ask the Holy Spirit to come and fill, empower, encourage fruit and give gifts. Get the group to pray for each other in small groups with a leader present in each group. Encourage them to share if a particular gift is wanted, then pray together. Afterwards in your small groups share what prayers were said/requests made. Keep the atmosphere of worship alive, you may want to continue to sing songs, play a worship tape etc.

Be sensitive to what is going on and only then decide how best to close the session. Be sure to follow up on this session through one-to-one contact. Encourage the young people who received a gift (tongues, prophecy etc) and give them opportunities to exercise this gift in a supportive situation.

# THE HOLY SPIRIT

1) Read Galatians 5:22-26 and write on the bunch of grapes opposite what the different 'fruit of the Spirit' are.

2) Read 1 Corinthians 12:4-11 and write one of the gifts of the Spirit on the boxes below.

### Don't forget!

'I may speak in different languages of people or even angels. But if I do not have love, I am only a noisy bell or a crashing cymbal. I may have the gift of prophecy. I may understand all the secret things of God and have all knowledge, and I may have faith so great that I can move mountains. But even with all these things, if I do not have love, then I am nothing' (1 Corinthians 13:1-2).

# WE ARE FAMILY

## MEETING AIM:
To teach that the church is a 'family' of believers, and to encourage involvement in and attendance at church services.

## MEETING PREPARATION
Recruit some church members to come to your youth group/club meeting to act as 'welcomers' and 'guides' to the church building. Brief these people thoroughly beforehand so they know what you want of them. Contact the church leaders for permission to use the main church building/sanctuary. Also ask them if the youth group/club can take part in some of or take a whole meeting.

## WELCOME TO THE FAMILY (10 mins)
Hold this meeting in your church building (most groups/clubs meet in a separate hall, room or home). Arrange for church members to be at the door to welcome the young people as they arrive and then mingle with them. You might want to have some light refreshments available to encourage a relaxed atmosphere.

Have a cassette player on hand repeatedly playing 'We are Family' by Sister Sledge as the young people arrive, or even better put this through the church PA (if you have one).

## CHURCH TOUR (10-15 mins)
Get the church members to take small groups of young people (maximum six) on a guided tour of the inside and outside of your church building. Obviously some churches have more historical interest than others, but concentrate on explaining why the pulpit, altar/communion table, baptistery/font are in the places they are. Usually one of these components is in the most dominant geographical position. This links to the theology of your church (ie, churches that put great emphasis on the preaching of scripture usually have the pulpit in the most commanding position). Encourage questions and feedback.

Bring everyone back together and ask them to describe the 'vibes' that the church building gives them (eg, warm, homely, creepy, ancient).

**SAY:** 'People often gauge their opinion of a church by the look of the building, but is that what the church actually is? Later we will look at what a church is and should be, but first a game...'

## EVERY SECOND COUNTS (10 mins)
This version of the TV gameshow *Every Second Counts* is a bit of fun and illustrates the large number of local churches mentioned in the New Testament. Ideally the quiz master should be male, middle-aged, vertically challenged and balding - in other words, look like Paul Daniels.

Four contestants take it in turns to respond to a possible name of a New Testament church, announced by the quiz master with either - *'It's a fellowship, Paul'* - (if they think the name is genuine),

OR

*'It's a figment, Paul'* - (if they think it isn't).

The four contestants answer in turn. If they answer correctly they stay in the game, score a point and the next question goes to the next contestant - and so on. When a contestant gets an answer wrong they drop out. (Drape a tea towel over their head.)

The last contestant left wins - carrying on as long as they keep getting the answers right, or until you run out of church names.

Mix up the two lists of genuine and fictitious churches below.

| 'FELLOWSHIP' | 'FICTION' |
| --- | --- |
| **Athens** (Acts 17:16f) | **Agamemnon** |
| **Antioch** (Acts 13:1) | **Epiglottis** |
| **Berea** (Acts 17:10f) | **Dettol** |
| **Corinth** (1 Corinthians 1:2) | **Ibiza** |
| **Ephesus** (Ephesians 1:1) | **Iota** |
| **Troas** (Acts 20:5f) | **Troy** |
| **Sardis** (Revelation 3:1) | **Tardis** |
| **Philippi** (Philippians 1:1) | **Trolop** |
| **Azotus** (Acts 8:40) | **Serdar** |
| **Sharon** (Acts 9:35f) | **Tracey** |
| **Derbe** (Acts 14:6) | **Epsom** |
| **Rome** (Romans 1:7) | **Moscow** |
| **Thyatira** (Revelation 2:18) | **Thyroid** |
| **Syracuse** (Acts 28:12) | **Smirnoff** |
| **Malta** (Acts 28:1) | **Majorca** |
| **Sidon** (Acts 27:3) | **Leadon** |
| **Philadelphia** (Revelation 3:7) | **Manitoba** |
| **Perga** (Acts 13:13) | **Chronicula** |
| **Rhegium** (Acts 28:13) | **Sydium** |

## THE FIRST CHURCH (15 mins)
**SAY:** 'Let's read about the first ever church to see how it worshipped together and attracted new believers.'

**READ OUT LOUD:** Acts 2:36-47. Explain that the first church didn't have its own building, but met in the Jewish temple or in each others' homes. There are still churches today which meet in homes or rented rooms/buildings/school halls. They lived together like a large extended family, sharing things and caring for each other. Then as Christianity spread, more and more communities of believers or churches started up. So instead of one church which met in Jerusalem, there were churches in lots of other towns and cities.

**DISCUSS:** What marked out the first Christians as different from other people? Why is it that each Christian church is slightly different? What are the similarities and differences between the description of the first church and this church? What similarities are there between a church and a family?

## SPOT THE CHRISTIAN (10 mins)
Hand out a copy of the worksheet opposite to each individual. Give them three minutes to complete the sheet and then compare answers.

**SAY:** 'Many people have a mental picture of a Christian as being someone who is old or a bit out of date. The fact is that every single person opposite could be a Christian! The church is made up of all sorts of different people.'

## CHURCH PLUG (15 mins)
Divide into small groups of three and ask each group to devise a 30-second TV advert about the church. The ad should include details about what the church is like, particular services/meetings of interest to various types of people, and above all 'sell' the church to the viewer. Give the groups 10 minutes to devise their ad which can be acted, sung (using a jingle), read, use captions or slogans etc. Then get each group in turn to perform their ad to the rest.

Discuss which ad was the most truthful, the most appealing, the most entertaining, etc. Pick up on some of the statements and slogans to delve into the young people's opinions and observations of church.

It could be good to get the adult 'welcomers' to stay and take part in this exercise and to compare their ad with the young people's. This could illustrate the different things people look for in a church.

## FAMILY GET-TOGETHERS (5 mins)
Read Hebrews 10:24-25 and then invite the young people to a suitable service. Ideally it should include them, hence the request to the church leaders for input from your group.

# SPOT THE CHRISTIAN!

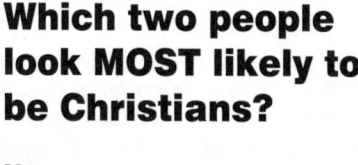

**Which two people look MOST likely to be Christians?**

No.....................

Why?..................
........................
........................
........................
........................
........................
........................
........................

No.....................

Why?..................
........................
........................
........................
........................
........................
........................
........................

**Which two people look LEAST likely to be Christians?**

No.....................

Why?..................
........................
........................
........................
........................
........................
........................
........................

No.....................

Why?..................
........................
........................
........................
........................
........................
........................
........................

# WORLD BEST-SELLER

## MEETING AIM:
To discover individuals' views and beliefs about the Bible. To begin to challenge popular misconceptions, stimulate interest in and explain the importance of reading scripture.

## BLIND COOKING (10 mins)

You will need the following props to run this crowdbreaker: 2 liquidisers, 2 bananas, one pint of milk, two teaspoons of lemon juice, 2oz of ground almonds, two glace cherries, 20ml of single cream, 30ml of treacle, two sardine/anchovy or sild, two slices of cucumber, 2oz of semi-crushed flake chocolate, two straws, plus two bottles each of the following sauces: chocolate, strawberry, caramel/toffee, cherry.

Divide the ingredients/props into two identical selections on a large table. Plug the liquidisers into an electric socket. Ensure that anyone using this has clear instructions on its safe and proper use. This avoids accidents and mess!

Explain to the young people that the opening activity is a contest to discover who can make the most delicious milkshake. Get two volunteer makers/tasters. Explain that two lots of identical ingredients to choose from are laid out on the table.

Once the two volunteers come forward, explain that you only have one recipe card with instructions on how to make a delicious bananachoc milkshake. Toss a coin to decide which person gets the recipe card. To the person that loses, explain that apart from milk and a banana they may as well choose the other ingredients with a blindfold on since they don't know the recipe. Then quickly blindfold the person and guide them along their ingredients from which they choose six elements. Once selected take the blindfold off and give both contestants up to two minutes to blend and whisk a tasty milkshake.

Encourage both contestants to sip some of their creation and then hand it round the group for anyone else brave or thirsty enough to try some!

At the end make the point that one contestant had a large advantage because they had the recipe which gave them expert advice on the right combination to make the best possible use of the ingredients. Introduce today's theme by saying that you believe it is possible to have a similar advantage in life by using the maker's instructions for living. If he made us and wrote a recipe book for living the best way, it must be worth checking out!

### BANANA-CHOC MILKSHAKE RECIPE
Blend a peeled banana and one teaspoon of lemon juice for 15 seconds. Add ½ pint milk, 10ml of cream and a desert spooon of chocolate sauce. Blend together for 30 seconds and pour into a tall glass. Cut a line from the centre of a slice of cucumber to the edge, then put the slice over the lip of the glass. Crumble a small amount of crushed chocolate flake onto the froth of the shake and its ready to drink with a straw!

## IN OR OUT (10 mins)

Many people misquote the Bible. Dot Cotton who used to appear in the BBC soap *Eastenders* was always mangling and misquoting scripture. Read out the quotes below and at the same time put the quote on a card or OHP. Allow three second's thinking time, then ask everyone to shout 'in' if they think it is a genuine quote from scripture, or 'out' if they think it isn't.

1) In the beginning God created the sky and the earth - **IN** *(Genesis 1:1)*
2) God helps those who help themselves - **OUT**
3) Cleanliness is next to godliness - **OUT**
4) You must not steal - **IN** *(Exodus 20:15)*
5) There is a time for everything - **IN** *(Ecclesiastes 3:1)*
6) Everyone is equal under the sun - **OUT**
7) Father forgive them, because they don't know what they are doing - **IN** *(Luke 23:34)*
8) For what we are about to receive may the Lord make us truly thankful - **OUT**
9) Money is the root of all evil - **OUT** ('the love of money' is described as the root of all evil in *1 Timothy 6:10*)
10) Hell hath no fury like a woman scorned - **OUT** (Shakespeare, not scripture!)
11) Don't judge other people, or you will be judged - **IN** *(Matthew 7:1)*
12) Turn or burn - **OUT**
13) Do all you can to lead a peaceful life - **IN** *(1 Thessalonians 4:11)*
14) He who would valiant be, against all disaster - **OUT** (popular school hymn written by John Bunyan)
15) Do not be fooled: you can't cheat God - **IN** *(Galatians 6:7)*

## 20 QUESTIONS (20+ mins)

Hand out photocopies of the 20 Questions tick sheet (opposite) and a pen/pencil. Allow up to five minutes for the sheets to be completed by individuals. Then comes the tricky part!

As the group share their answers it is important to allow people to have their own views but at the same time ask appropriate questions to get behind the reasons why they answered as they did. This applies just as much to Christians who gave very 'positive' answers.

Carefully prepare questions beforehand that will get people talking and discussing their answers. Use *Why, When, How, If* type questions that cannot be answered by a simple 'yes' or 'no'.

Note that questions 11 to 16 are illustrated by the selected readings listed at the end of the 'Right Riveting Read' section.

## RIGHT RIVETING READ (20 mins)

Select a member of the group, one of the leaders or a member of the church congregation to talk for a maximum of five minutes about their favourite passage/story from scripture. They need to say why it's their favourite and how it has spoken to/challenged/encouraged/surprised them. And of course, they should also read out the passage (from a modern translation), up to a maximum of 20 verses.

Then ask the young people what their favourite 'bits' from the Bible are and why.

Explain that the word 'Bible' comes from the Greek word *biblia* meaning 'books', and that this collection of 66 books took many different people over 1,000 years to write.

Conclude this session by reading out the following verses from the Bible, some of which will be familiar to them, others may surprise:

'**The Lord is my shepherd; I have everything I need**' *Psalm 23:1*, (famous poetry).

'**When the Levite got home, he took a knife and cut his slave woman into twelve parts, limb by limb. Then he sent a part to each part of Israel**' *Judges 19:29*, (historical accounts of lawless frontier days of Old Testament Israel).

'**My lover's left arm is under my head, and his right arm holds me tight**' *Song of Soloman 8:3*, (song celebrating sexual love).

'If you loudly greet your neighbour early in the morning, he will think of it as a curse' *Proverbs 27:14,* (practical tips on living).

'Whoever says that he lives in God must live as Jesus lived' *1 John 2:6,* (a call to a radical alternative lifestyle).

'God loved the world so much that he gave his one and only Son so that whoever believes in him may not be lost, but have eternal life' *John 3:16,* (the main theme of the Bible: God's plan to save the human race from sin and death through Jesus Christ).

## CRUCIAL READING (5 mins)

Read 2 Timothy 3:14-17, then say: 'This part of the Bible was written by St Paul to his friend Timothy to encourage him in his Christian faith. Timothy had learned about Jesus from childhood. Paul explains why he thinks reading the scriptures is so important - because it is inspired by God and is more than just a good read or wise sayings, but actually a guidebook for living from God himself.'

Display a range of modern translations/paraphrases of the Bible for your group to look at. As well as different translations, also have some of the newer editions available which are specifically aimed at young people. These Bibles include useful 'helps' and notes which make them an excellent buy.

Particularly recommended are: [NIV] The Insight Bible (Hodders); [Living Bible] The Student Bible (Kingsway); and [New Century Version] The Youth Bible (Word), which in its paperback format is the only Bible I have seen with the word 'sex' on the front cover!

## OPTIONAL EXTRAS

### BIBLE TRIVIA GAME

There are a host of different Bible trivia games available. Your local Christian bookshop will stock a range, or you may find someone in your church would lend you theirs. If your group have a fairly good level of Bible knowledge a Bible Trivial Pursuits evening will be both fun and instructive. Alternatively, for groups with less Bible knowledge, you could write your own questions geared to them. These could be based on the teaching content in the group over the past few weeks/term/year.

Scriptures quoted from The Youth Bible, New Century Version (Anglicised Edition) © 1993 by Nelson Word Ltd, 9 Holdom Ave, Bletchley, Milton Keynes MK1 1QR.

# 20 Questions

Give your honest opinions to the following statements by ticking either the 'Agree' (A) or 'Disagree' (D) boxes.

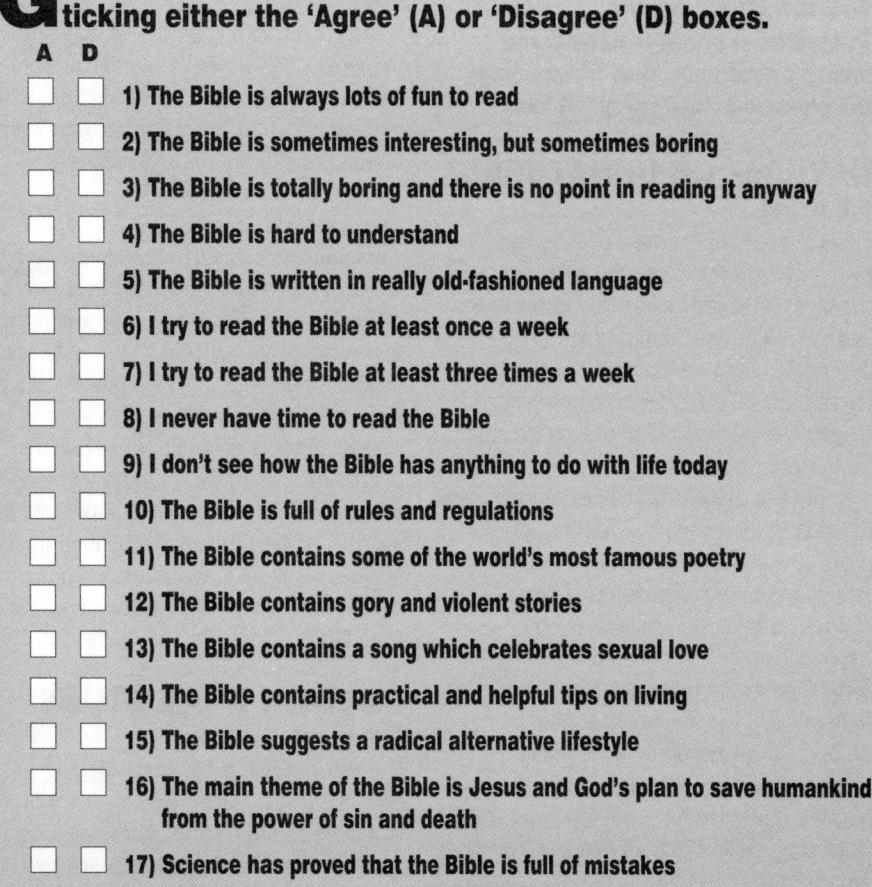

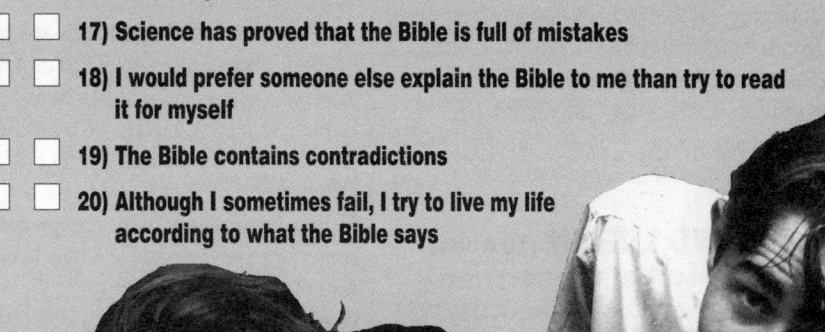

A  D

1) The Bible is always lots of fun to read
2) The Bible is sometimes interesting, but sometimes boring
3) The Bible is totally boring and there is no point in reading it anyway
4) The Bible is hard to understand
5) The Bible is written in really old-fashioned language
6) I try to read the Bible at least once a week
7) I try to read the Bible at least three times a week
8) I never have time to read the Bible
9) I don't see how the Bible has anything to do with life today
10) The Bible is full of rules and regulations
11) The Bible contains some of the world's most famous poetry
12) The Bible contains gory and violent stories
13) The Bible contains a song which celebrates sexual love
14) The Bible contains practical and helpful tips on living
15) The Bible suggests a radical alternative lifestyle
16) The main theme of the Bible is Jesus and God's plan to save humankind from the power of sin and death
17) Science has proved that the Bible is full of mistakes
18) I would prefer someone else explain the Bible to me than try to read it for myself
19) The Bible contains contradictions
20) Although I sometimes fail, I try to live my life according to what the Bible says

PHOTO: JIM LORING

# PRAYER

**MEETING AIM:**
To teach that prayer is natural and makes a difference. Also to encourage the group to actually pray out loud.

## NATURAL OR UNNATURAL?
**(15 mins)**

Hand out pens and a sheet of A5 paper to everyone. Ask them to write the word 'natural' at the top of one side of the page, and the word 'unnatural' at the top of the other side. Then ask the group to compile a list of things they regard as natural, eg laughter, thirst; and unnatural, eg exhaust fumes, plastic flowers.

Allow five minutes and then ask for people to read out their lists. Use a flip chart or write on an OHP to compile a master list. Allow some discussion/debate over controversial or questionable entries.

It may be that some people have suggested some God-aware/religious qualities on their 'natural' list. Conclude this section by saying that many people would regard prayer as a natural element, not least because it is something that everyone does at some stage in their life. When new people groups have been 'discovered' by Western civilisation, the people/tribe always have a god or gods which they attempted to communicate with. This in a nutshell is what prayer is - communicating with God.

## TALK AND LISTEN (10 mins)

Divide the group into pairs. One person is the talker, the other is the listener. Get the talkers to stand on one side of the room, with the listeners standing opposite their partner on the other side of the room.

Listeners each receive a pad of paper and a pen and are told to write down word for word what the talker says.

The talkers are each given a different book (it can be anything from a DIY manual to a technical text book; a best-selling novel to a biography). Ask them to open the book at random and start reading at a slow enough pace for the listeners to write down what they say.

If you have less fewer than five pairs, switch on a radio which is tuned in to a speech programme, eg, BBC Radio 4. This will add some distracting background interference, making the listener's job more difficult. If you have five pairs or more, the hubbub from all those raised voices will be distracting enough without additional interference.

After about three minutes of mayhem, call things to a halt. Then get the listeners to read back to the talkers what they recorded. Pick out one or two to be read out to everyone, highlighting the errors and misheard elements of the message.

Conclude this exercise by saying that communication is a tricky business. What we say to someone can be misheard or misunderstood. But what about when we try to communicate with God, or God tries to communicate with us? This process can be just as difficult sometimes.

**ASK:** What sort of things provide the interference when we try to pray to God? What stops us from praying? How can God possibly understand all the different prayer messages that he must get each minute of the day? What can stop us hearing right from God?

## SWEDISH BIBLE STUDY
**(20 mins)**

Use the Swedish Bible study method to examine Jesus' teaching on prayer. For this you will need to photocopy the card with symbols below. Enlarge the image by 100%.

As a group read together Luke 11:1-13, then hand out a card and pen to everyone. Explain that they need to go over the passage and next to each symbol do the following:

■ Beside the arrow pointing upwards write something these verses teach us about Jesus/God.
■ Beside the arrow pointing downwards write something these verses teach about humankind.
■ Beside the lightbulb write some new insight or discovery you have made from reading these verses.
■ Beside the exclamation mark write what is the most exciting verse in your opinion and why.
■ Beside the question mark write anything you didn't understand or want to ask about.
■ Beside the arrow pointing sideways write down something which these verses say we should do.

**N.B.** *You may need to repeat these instructions several times. Also make sure everyone has access to a Bible.*

Allow 8-10 minutes for the Swedish Bible study, then ask for people to feedback. Ask for everyone's response to the first symbol before moving on to the next answer.

Emphasise that prayer can be hard work, but very rewarding, so we need to be persistent. You may want to give a short three-minute 'prayer changes things' talk with examples from your life of answered prayer, plus what you learned from situations where your prayer was not answered in the way you wanted/expected.

## NEWSPRAYER (5 mins)

Conclude by splitting into small groups for the Prayer Diary exercise right, or alternatively show a video recording of that day's television news headlines, or select three or four headlines from the newspapers and photocopy them onto an OHP acetate or simply stick them on a cork board.

If you have a group which are anxious about praying out loud, ask them to write a prayer about one of the news subjects and then in turn read them out. Alternatively, get them in a circle and ask them to take turns to pray a one-sentence prayer.

## PRAYER DIARY

Hand out copies of the prayer diary sheet opposite and ask people to get together in groups of three (this may need to be carefully overseen to ensure people are not left out - groups of two or four are acceptable, but not preferable).

Either at the meeting or in their own time, encourage the small groups to meet as prayer triplets at least once a week for 15 minutes, to list prayer needs and answers using the prayer diary sheet.

You could use this as part of your ongoing programme over the next few weeks.

Be sure to speak to at least one person from each small group over the next few weeks to encourage them to pray together.

# Prayer Diary

| Date | Prayer details | Date | Answer details |
|------|----------------|------|----------------|
|      |                |      |                |

'Do not worry about anything, but pray and ask God for everything you need, always giving thanks' (Philippians 4:6).

'Pray in the spirit at all times with all kinds of prayers, asking for everything you need. To do this you must always be ready and never give up. Always pray for all God's people (Ephesians' 6:18).

| Date | Prayer details | Date | Answer details |
|------|----------------|------|----------------|
|      |                |      |                |

'Pray for all rulers and for all who have authority' (1 Timothy 2:1-2).

# FORGIVENESS

**MEETING AIM:**
To teach that God is willing to forgive us, but this is conditional on us forgiving others.

## THE SIN BIN (15 mins)

Begin this session with a contact sports game such as uni-hock, basketball or 5-a-side soccer. At the first foul blow a whistle to stop the game and tell the person who committed the foul to apologise. Then ask the person who was fouled if he/she accepts the apology. If they say 'yes', award them a free kick/hit/shot. If they say 'no', as well as awarding the free kick/hit/shot, take out a red card and order the player who committed the foul off to the 'sin bin' for 5 minutes/or the rest of the game.

Explain to the person who committed the offence that you are doing this because the other player refused to accept his/her apology.

Once the first player gets sent off in this way, the other players are likely to continue to refuse to apologise when they get fouled and the game will descend into farce with less and less players left actually playing, and most on the sidelines.

At the end of the game, explain that the theme this week is forgiveness. Point out that a lack of forgiveness in the game removed the purpose and pleasure of the game, once the initial humour of the situation was gone.

## IS SORRY ENOUGH? (25 mins)

Hand everyone a photocopy of the sheet opposite. Read out the story of Kirsty and Amber and allow up to 5 minutes for people to write their response. Then get the group to read out their answers. Without taking sides, stimulate a discussion on the issue of forgiveness. Develop the arguments raised and take people's reactions further (eg Kirsty's justifiable anger may result in the end of a friendship, which in the long term could hurt Kirsty as much or more than Amber).

Encourage your young people to draw on personal examples of friends breaking promises and falling out or making up. Many young people go through this process on a regular basis, so you may find that 25 minutes is nothing like enough time for this section.

## NEWSPAPER BINGO (5 mins)

Divide your group into two or more equal teams (maximum four in a team). Give each group a pile of newspapers (minimum six per team), a pen and a newspaper bingo card (see example below). You could make up your own card if you prefer. The winning team is the one which can rip out of its papers stories which have examples of all of the categories on the bingo card. If at the end of five minutes no team has shouted 'full house', the winner is the team with most categories ticked.

At the end of the game make the point that our newspapers are full of stories of people who have been wronged by others. When we are wronged, once we get over the initial shock/pain we are faced with a choice: to bear a grudge and become bitter about that person, or to forgive them and begin to put it behind us.

Ask: Why is it often hard to forgive?

## FORGIVE US AS WE FORGIVE OTHERS (10+ mins)

Read 1 Timothy 1:12-17 then briefly explain how Paul had persecuted the early Christians until he was dramatically confronted by the power and reality of the risen Christ. He then became a follower of Jesus and went to those he formerly persecuted to work with and alongside them to spread the gospel.

Paul had to say 'sorry' to God and the Christians. The Christians could have rejected his apology and not allowed Paul any contact with them, but they chose to forgive him. Underline that the history of the church would have been crucially different if the early Christians had rejected Paul the new convert who wanted forgiveness.

Play some appropriate music on a cassette player or sing some worship songs which focus on the theme of forgiveness and getting right with God.

During this time ask the group to consider carefully whether there is a person or situation in which they need to ask God (and others) for forgiveness. Also ask them to consider whether they are holding a grudge against someone who has wronged them. Stress that Jesus taught that if we fail to forgive others, God cannot forgive us. It may be appropriate to pray together the Lord's Prayer at this point - using it as a vehicle to ask God's forgiveness and to forgive others.

Encourage members within the group to get right with each other there and then or as soon as possible.

## OPTIONAL EXTRAS

### THE HIDING PLACE

Show part or all of the film 'The Hiding Place', the true story of Corrie ten Boom and her family who sheltered Jews in occupied Holland during World War II. When Corrie and her sister were sent to a concentration camp, their Christian faith and ability to forgive the evil camp wardens were stretched to the limit. This feature length video is available for sale or rent from many Christian bookshops, or in case of difficulty contact: International Films, c/o Scripture Press, Raans Road, Amersham, Bucks HP6 6JQ. Tel: 0494 722151.

## NEWSPAPER BINGO

| Adultery | Murder | Slander | Racism |
|---|---|---|---|
| Fraud/Cheating | Broken promise | Unkind act | Sexism |
| Thoughtlessness | Sexual crime | Burglary | Cruelty |

# IS SORRY ENOUGH?

Amber and Kirsty had been best friends for over a year. They got on so well and had such a similar attitude to life that many people thought they must be twins. They had the same taste in clothes, boys and music. In particular they both liked 'The Grifters' who had just announced the dates for their European tour.

Amber and Kirsty had been listening to The Grifters for ages, even before they had become a well-known band. They had all their albums and had been making plans to buy tickets at the one and only British concert date for the latest Grifters tour. It meant a very early start to catch the 5.48am train to get to town early enough to be sure of a ticket when they went on sale at 9am.

On the big day, Kirsty was at the station by 5.30, but by 5.45 there was still no sign of Amber. As the train arrived at the station Kirsty frantically ran out of the entrance to see if her friend was running up the road, but there was no sign of her. Kirsty turned round in time to see the train leaving the platform - now she had missed the train too!

According to the timetable there wasn't another train for an hour, so Kirsty walked to Amber's house a mile away and knocked on the door. It took ages for anyone to answer, and then when the door opened it was Amber's dad. He wasn't too pleased at being woken up early.

Amber eventually opened her bedroom door. 'I thought we agreed to meet at the station in time for the first train,' said an angry Kirsty.

'Oh sorry, I must've overslept,' said Amber. But Kirsty didn't think she looked very sorry.

'If you got there on time you should have caught the train without me,' said Amber. 'Oh well, if you catch the next train you can still get there before the ticket office opens. Get an extra ticket for me, will you?' she added.

Kirsty hit the roof and started shouting at Amber about breaking her promise and how she could buy her own ticket. Amber yawned and apologised again while rubbing her eyes. Kirsty stormed out of the house.

Although Kirsty caught the 6.48 train, by the time she got to the ticket office at 8.30 the queue was enormous. At about 10am it started to rain. At 11.15 the queue had progressed so that Kirsty had only about 30 people in front of her. By then she had decided to buy only one ticket. It would serve Amber right!

Then a man announced that all the tickets were sold, so could everyone please leave?

Without a ticket and having wasted a whole morning and the price of the train fare; having got wet and cold, and worst of all been let down by her friend, Kirsty felt miserable on the journey home. As she sat on the train she thought about Amber, her so-called friend. They were supposed to be meeting up tomorrow to go shopping. Then on Monday they normally walked to school together. Amber had said 'sorry' twice, but was that enough?

● Write down how you think Kirsty should react to this situation. Give reasons for your answer.

# ?DOUBTS?

## MEETING AIM:
To recognise that doubt is not necessarily shameful, but can be a positive force for growth in the Christian life. Also that doubts come from several sources, that they shouldn't frighten us - our God has the answers.

## STARTER OPTIONS

Here are two attention-grabbing ways to start the evening:

**1.** Start with a fairly boring, lengthy, spoken introduction. Suddenly a stranger crashes through the door, points a starting pistol at you, shoots and runs off. When people have calmed down again, ask them to write a description of the stranger. They saw him - but because the experience was so out of the ordinary, a lot of their ideas will be extremely unclear. Just like becoming a Christian, really.

**2.** When people arrive, the place is locked and in darkness. Have you forgotten to turn up? Is it the wrong night? Has it been cancelled? Keep them hanging about until they've almost decided to give up and go home. Then let them in - but use the experience to launch a discussion of how it feels to be in a state of doubt about what's going on...

## INSTANT VOTE (5 mins)

Ask people to respond to each of these statements. If they are absolutely convinced that they are true, they should stand up and cheer loudly. If they are undecided, they should sit still and scratch their heads, and if they are pretty sure the statement is false, they should lean forward, scowl and shake their heads slowly.

1) Edinburgh is further north than Moscow.
2) Manchester United will win the European Cup.
3) The next total eclipse of the sun occurs in Britain during 1996.
4) There is life on other planets.
5) The earliest-surviving cigarette packet dates from 1860.
6) The capital city of Mongolia is called Mongo.
7) Billy Graham's middle name is Franklin.
8) The youth leader is a complete idiot.
9) The Body Shop never advertises.
10) Tomorrow something great is going to happen.

*(1,5,7 and 9 are all correct.)*

Analyse what happened. There are different reasons for uncertainty: because you don't know the facts; because nobody knows; or because it's a matter of opinion. Why do Christians sometimes find themselves uncertain about their faith?

## DIAGNOSIS (15 mins)

The first thing is to establish what we know about doubts. Divide into three groups. Ask one to answer the *difficult questions* which often cause doubts (eg: Can you trust the Bible? Did the resurrection happen?).

Another should list the *puzzling circumstances* which cause doubts (eg why your girlfriend is dying of cancer; when your prayers aren't being answered). Ask the third to list the *personal causes* there can be (eg feeling let down by Christians; feeling discouraged by the power of temptation).

Check the lists and discuss:
**1)** Which of these, in your experience is the biggest problem of all?
**2)** Do doubts start suddenly or grow over a period of time?
**3)** Are these causes of doubt all separate, or do they ever overlap?

Then say: 'Human beings aren't just bodies, and aren't just minds. Spirit, soul and body are all interlinked, so when doubts come, they won't always be rational, logical, intellectual problems. Their strength may derive from damaged emotions or a weakened body.'

Paul Little in his book, *How To Give Away Your Faith* (IVP), claims that most people can come up with only seven basic objections to the Christian faith - and there are answers to all of them! So we shouldn't be worried that Christianity will let us down intellectually. Doubts aren't fatal.

## POSITIVE AND NEGATIVE (15 mins)

Play a game in two teams. One team ties a piece of red wool on each member's left arm; the other team uses blue. People run around and the blues try to pull off the red armbands within a five-minute limit. The reds are allowed to take evasive action, but must not fight back or remove the blue armbands.

Then play the game again with a difference. This time both teams are trying to pull off the other's armbands within the five-minute limit.

Discuss how different it felt playing the second way - especially for the reds! You're much more likely to do well if you can positively go on the attack, instead of just negatively running away.

Explain that this applies to our doubts too. Many people react negatively when they have doubts - they stuff them down into their subconscious and try to forget them (like the blue team!) they don't go away - they just press harder. Positive doubting means dragging your feelings out into the open and looking at them fearlessly. Why are you doubting? What's the state of the evidence? Are there answers to your questions you haven't explored?

## GREAT BIBLICAL DOUBTERS (20 mins)

Hand out copies of the report sheets (opposite) and work through the biblical passages, filling it in. Feedback, then make the points:
**1)** Some of God's greatest servants had doubts - to doubt God isn't shameful or immature.
**2)** There are obvious causes for the doubts in each case. These things are recorded so that we will be warned!
**3)** God doesn't condemn his doubting servants, but he does supply answers to help them.

## WRAP UP (5 mins)

Give people a moment to think about (maybe even write down) the three biggest doubt-producers in their own lives. When they have their list, let them think through what action they need to take to deal with them positively rather than letting them fester negatively. Finally, stress again the main points you've made on the way through, and end by praying together.

## OPTIONAL EXTRAS

Many young Christians have never seriously examined the basis of their faith. Have some good short books and booklets available on the spot for them to borrow afterwards, to look at the evidence for Christian belief.

Particularly recommended is *Good Questions* - a cassette or video by Steve Chalke (Scripture Union), and *It Makes Sense* by Stephen Gaukgroger (Scripture Union).

| NAME | UNDERLYING REASON FOR DOUBTS | WHAT DID THIS PERSON DOUBT? | WHAT HAPPENED? |
|---|---|---|---|
| **ELIJAH** 1 Kings 19:3-18 | | | |
| **THOMAS** John 20:24-29 | | | |
| **GIDEON** Judges 6:1-16 | | | |
| **AARON** Exodus 32:1-9 | | | |

# YOUTHWORK

## READY-TO-USE MEETING GUIDE 10

Creative and fun session plans with photocopiable activity worksheets

### VOLUME 1: CHRISTIAN BASICS

John Buckeridge

**HELP YOUTH**
- Discover faith
- Examine the Bible
- Explore prayer
- Learn to forgive
- Deal with doubts

**A WHOLE TERM'S WORTH OF:**
- Games
- Discussion starters
- Talks
- Copy-free worksheets
- Bible studies
- Icebreakers
- Optional extras

# Further titles in the YOUTHWORK Ready-To-Use Meeting Guide series:

**Volume 2** - LIFESTYLE includes meeting plans on self esteem, sex, money, hypocrisy and caring for creation. Published November 1994.

**Volume 3** - CULTURE includes meeting plans on television, drugs, adverts, music and New Age. Due to be published March 1995.

**Volume 4** - BELIEF includes meeting plans on death and resurrection, temptation, evangelism, miracles and apologetics. Due to be published October 1995.

Available from your local Christian bookshop or direct from Kingsway on freephone 0800 378446.

*From the person who wrote this book...*

# YEAR-ROUND HELP FOR YOUTH WORKERS/LEADERS

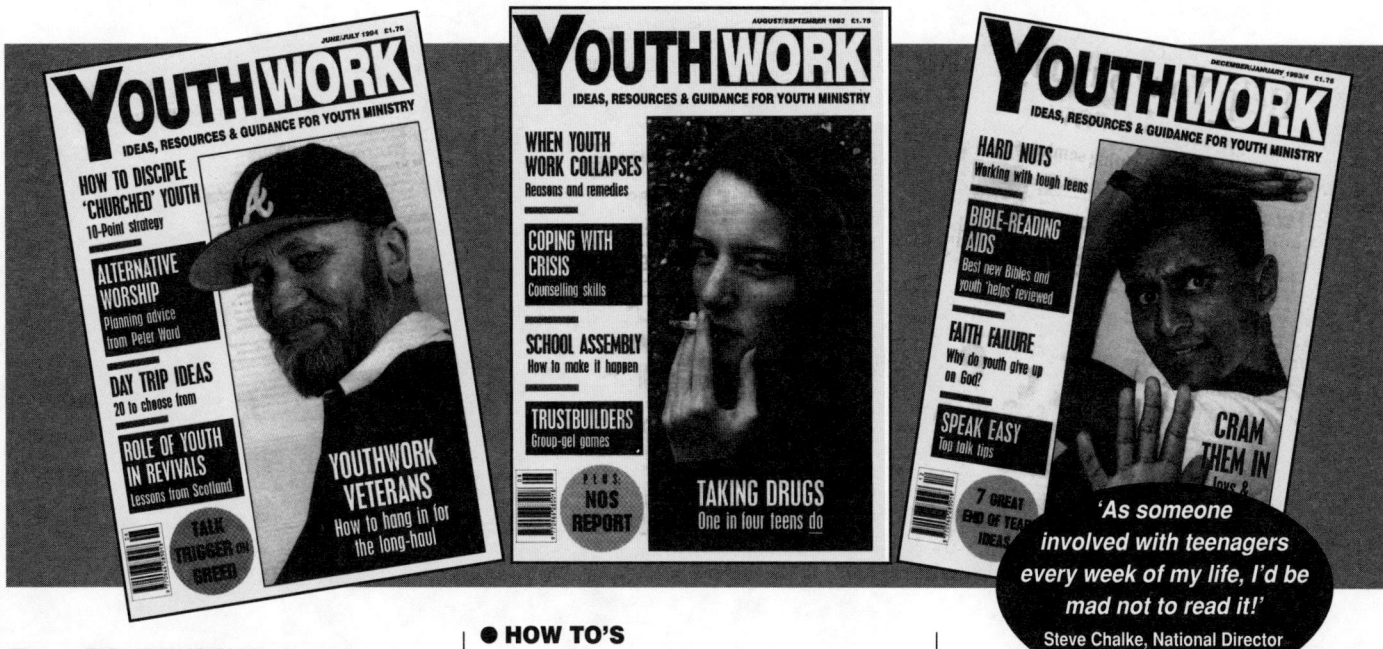

*'As someone involved with teenagers every week of my life, I'd be mad not to read it!'*
Steve Chalke, National Director of Oasis Trust

**Y**OUTH**WORK** is the magazine for all Christians actively involved in youth ministry. Edited by John Buckeridge, this bi-monthly magazine is full of practical ideas and resources for youth workers/leaders.

YOUTH**WORK** is crammed with...

● **IDEAS, IDEAS & YET MORE IDEAS**
Games, icebreakers, discussion starters, theme nights, all night lock-ins, evangelistic projects, ready-to-use meetings etc.

● **HOW TO'S**
Practical and comprehensive 'how to's' on the nuts and bolts of youth work. From programme planning to starting from scratch, organising an evangelistic event to communication skills.

● **YOUTH TRENDS**
What's going on, who started it and what does it mean? Youth culture examined and analysed, plus a regular culture quiz to test your street cred testing!

● **PASTORAL ISSUES**
Discipling unchurched converts, counselling teens in crisis, accountability to church leaders, young people & the law etc.

● **RESOURCE REVIEW**
In every issue we review and analyse the latest books, videos and other new resources available for youth work.

● **HEADSCRATCHERS**
Articles to make even the busiest youth worker stop and think through the theory and practice of youth ministry.

## TAKE OUT A 2-YEAR SUBSCRIPTION AND SAVE £2.50

Complete this coupon and post to: YOUTH**WORK**, FREEPOST, 37 Elm Road, New Malden, Surrey KT3 3BR.

☐ I want to take out a one-year subscription to YOUTH**WORK** magazine. Enclosed is my payment of £12.75*.

☐ I want to SAVE £2.50 by taking out a two-year subscription to YOUTH**WORK** magazine. Enclosed is my payment of £23.00*.

☐ I want to SAVE £5 by taking out a new one-year subscription to YOUTH**WORK** and ALPHA magazine for the combined price of £31.45*.

Name........................................ MB1
Address....................................
..............................................
.........................Postcode............

1. I enclose a cheque for £.................* made payable to Elm House Christian Communications Ltd.
2. Please debit my credit card account with £..................*
The Access ☐ Visa ☐ number is entered below
*Please complete

Signature........................ exp. date ☐☐/☐☐

If you prefer to obtain YOUTH**WORK** from your local Christian bookshop or church agent, hand this coupon to them to make sure of your copy.

To: Bookshop/Church Agent
Please reserve me ......... copies of YOUTH**WORK** until further notice.

Name........................................
Address....................................
..............................................
..............................................
..............................................

*These prices apply up to 1 April 1995. Following this date prices may vary. This price applies to UK subscribers. Not usable in conjunction with any other offers. Overseas subscribers please note: payable by sterling draft or credit card only. YOUTH**WORK** 1 year, Europe £17.50, Rest of the World £18.10; 2 years, Europe £32.50, Rest of the World £33.70; ALPHA/YOUTH**WORK** combined subscription Europe £43.20; Rest of the World £45.20. Elm House Christian Communications Ltd, 37 Elm Road, New Malden, Surrey KT3 3HB. Elm House Christian Communications Ltd is registered under the Data Protection Act 1980 and holds names and addresses on computer for the purpose of mailing in accordance with the terms registered under the Data Protection Act 1984. Details on request.
☐ Please tick here if you do not wish to receive promotional mailings from other companies.